Breaking Barriers:

Strategies for Conflict Resolution and Effective Communication

Asma

Breaking Barriers:

Strategies for Conflict Resolution and Effective Communication

Copyright © 2023 by Asma

This book is a work of fiction. Names, characters, places, and incidents either are the product of the author's imagination or are used fictitiously. Any resemblance to actual events, locales, persons, living or dead, is entirely coincidental.

The first edition was published in 2023

ISBN: 978-81-19747-67-2

Published by:
Ujwal
1663 Liberty Drive
Hyderabad, IN 47403
www.Ujwalublishers.com

This book is self-published using on-demand printing and publishing, which allows it to be printed and distributed globally.

Chapter 1: Introduction

The Importance of Conflict Resolution and Effective Communication

In our fast-paced, interconnected world, conflict is inevitable. Whether it's a disagreement with a coworker, a misunderstanding with a loved one, or a clash of opinions within a community, conflict can arise in various aspects of our lives. However, how we handle these conflicts and communicate our thoughts and feelings can make all the difference in maintaining healthy relationships and achieving our goals. This chapter explores the essential concepts of conflict resolution and effective communication, aiming to equip everyone with the necessary skills to navigate conflicts and communicate better in any situation.

Conflict resolution is not about avoiding or suppressing conflicts, but rather finding mutually beneficial solutions that address the underlying issues. It involves active listening, empathy, and a willingness to understand different perspectives. By acknowledging and addressing conflicts head-on, we can prevent them from escalating into more significant problems, fostering healthier relationships and positive outcomes.

Effective communication plays a pivotal role in conflict resolution. It is the foundation upon which conflicts can be resolved peacefully and relationships can be strengthened. Communication is not merely about the words we use but also about non-verbal cues, active listening, and emotional intelligence. This subchapter delves into the importance of clear and concise communication, active listening, and assertiveness in expressing thoughts and feelings without aggression.

Beyond conflict resolution, effective communication is a vital skill in various aspects of life. Whether in the workplace, interpersonal relationships, or even within ourselves, being able to communicate effectively can lead to better understanding, cooperation, and personal growth. This chapter provides practical strategies for improving communication skills, such as active listening exercises, conflict resolution role-plays, and tips for effective public speaking.

"Simply Said: Communicating Better at Work and Beyond" is a sub-niche that emphasizes the practical application of effective communication strategies in professional and personal settings. This chapter explores the unique challenges faced in the workplace and offers specific techniques to enhance communication among colleagues, superiors, and subordinates. It also highlights the importance of effective communication beyond the workplace, including in personal relationships, social interactions, and self-expression.

By mastering conflict resolution and effective communication, we can break barriers that hinder our personal and professional growth. This chapter aims to empower everyone, regardless of their background or expertise, with the knowledge and skills needed to navigate conflicts, communicate assertively, and build strong and meaningful connections. By investing in our communication skills, we can create a more harmonious and successful future for ourselves and those around us.

Chapter 2: Understanding Conflict

Definition and Types of Conflict

Conflict is an inherent part of human interaction. It arises when individuals or groups have differing interests, goals, values, or perspectives. While conflict often carries a negative connotation, it can also be a catalyst for growth, change, and improved relationships. In this subchapter, we will explore the definition and types of conflict to gain a better understanding of its nature and how it affects our lives.

Conflict can be defined as a struggle or disagreement between two or more parties who perceive incompatible goals or resources. It can occur in various settings, including personal relationships, workplaces, communities, and even within oneself. Understanding the types of conflict can help us navigate these situations more effectively.

One type of conflict is interpersonal conflict, which arises between individuals due to differences in personality, communication styles, or values. This type of conflict can be both overt and covert, and it often leads to strained relationships and unproductive interactions.

Another type of conflict is intrapersonal conflict, which occurs within an individual. It arises when a person experiences conflicting desires, beliefs, or emotions. Intrapersonal conflict can be challenging to resolve, as it requires self-reflection and introspection to identify and address the underlying issues.

Organizational conflict is yet another type that occurs within a workplace or any structured environment. It can arise from disagreements over power, authority, resources, or differing goals. Organizational conflict, if not effectively managed, can lead to decreased productivity, low morale, and a toxic work environment.

Lastly, societal conflict refers to conflicts that arise between different groups or communities within a society. These conflicts can be based on factors such as race, religion, ethnicity, or political beliefs. Managing societal conflict requires a collective effort to promote understanding, empathy, and open dialogue.

Understanding the types of conflict is crucial for effective conflict resolution and communication. By recognizing the different forms of conflict, one can develop strategies to address and resolve conflicts constructively. It is important to approach conflicts with an open mind, active listening, and a willingness to find common ground.

In conclusion, conflict is an inevitable part of human interaction. It can take various forms, including interpersonal, intrapersonal, organizational, and societal conflict. By understanding the nature of conflict and its different types, we can develop effective strategies for conflict resolution and better communication.

Causes and Effects of Conflict

Conflict is an inevitable part of human interactions, occurring in various settings such as workplaces, families, and even between nations. Understanding the causes and effects of conflict is crucial for effective communication and conflict resolution. In this subchapter, we will explore the key factors that give rise to conflicts and the profound impact they can have on individuals and relationships.

One of the primary causes of conflict is a lack of effective communication. Misunderstandings, misinterpretations, and miscommunication can quickly escalate into conflicts, creating a barrier to productive dialogue. Additionally, differing values, beliefs, and opinions can lead to disagreements, as individuals may struggle to find common ground. Cultural differences, varying communication styles, and language barriers can further exacerbate conflicts, highlighting the importance of developing cross-cultural communication skills.

Another significant cause of conflict is competition, whether it be for resources, power, or recognition. In highly competitive environments such as workplaces, conflicts can arise when individuals feel threatened or marginalized. These conflicts can impede collaboration, innovation, and overall team performance, underscoring the need for conflict resolution strategies.

The effects of conflict can be far-reaching and detrimental. In personal relationships, unresolved conflicts can lead to resentment, anger, and a breakdown of trust. This can erode the emotional connection between individuals and strain the bonds that hold relationships together. In professional settings, conflicts can result in decreased productivity, increased stress levels, and a toxic work environment. This not only affects individual well-being but can also impact the overall success of organizations.

Recognizing and addressing conflicts in a timely manner is crucial to prevent further escalation. Effective conflict resolution strategies, such as active listening, empathy, and compromise, can help bridge the gap between conflicting parties. Developing emotional intelligence, self-awareness, and assertiveness skills are also vital for managing conflicts constructively.

In conclusion, conflicts can arise from various causes, including communication breakdowns and competition. The effects of conflict can be detrimental to personal relationships and professional environments. By understanding the root causes of conflicts and implementing effective conflict resolution strategies, individuals can break down barriers, improve communication, and foster better relationships. Learning to navigate conflicts is a valuable skill that everyone should strive to develop, as it leads to more harmonious interactions and a more peaceful world.

Common Barriers to Conflict Resolution and Effective Communication

In today's fast-paced and interconnected world, effective communication and conflict resolution have become essential skills in all aspects of life. Whether it is in the workplace, personal relationships, or within communities, being able to communicate effectively and resolve conflicts is crucial for success and maintaining healthy relationships. However, there are several common barriers that often hinder these processes. Identifying and understanding these barriers is the first step towards breaking them down and achieving better communication and conflict resolution.

One of the most significant barriers to effective communication is a lack of active listening. In today's digital age, where distractions abound, people often find it challenging to truly listen and understand others. Instead, they may be preoccupied with their own thoughts, waiting for their turn to speak, or multitasking. Active listening involves giving undivided attention to the speaker, understanding their perspective, and responding appropriately. By practicing active listening, individuals can overcome this barrier and foster better communication.

Another common barrier is the use of vague or ambiguous language. Misunderstandings often arise when individuals fail to articulate their thoughts clearly or use jargon that is unfamiliar to others. This can lead to confusion, frustration, and even conflict. To overcome this barrier, it is crucial to use simple and concise language, avoid jargon or technical terms when talking to a diverse audience, and ask for clarification when needed.

Emotional barriers also play a significant role in hindering effective communication and conflict resolution. When individuals are overwhelmed by emotions such as anger, fear, or sadness, they may find it challenging to express themselves clearly or listen to others objectively. Emotions can cloud judgment and lead to misunderstandings or irrational reactions. It is essential to manage emotions effectively, remain calm, and create a safe space for open dialogue and understanding.

Cultural and language barriers can also impede effective communication and conflict resolution, especially in diverse settings. Differences in language, customs, and values can lead to misunderstandings and misinterpretations. It is crucial to embrace cultural diversity, foster inclusivity, and promote open-mindedness to overcome these barriers. Seeking to understand and appreciate different perspectives can lead to more effective communication and conflict resolution.

In conclusion, effective communication and conflict resolution are vital skills for success in all aspects of life. However, common barriers often hinder our ability to communicate and resolve conflicts effectively. By actively listening, using clear language, managing emotions, and embracing cultural diversity, we can break down these barriers and achieve better communication and conflict resolution. The journey towards effective communication and conflict resolution begins with recognizing and addressing these barriers, enabling us to build stronger relationships, both at work and beyond.

Chapter 3: Strategies for Conflict Resolution

Active Listening and Empathy

In today's fast-paced and interconnected world, effective communication has become more crucial than ever. Whether you are at work, home, or anywhere in between, mastering the art of active listening and empathy can greatly enhance your relationships and resolve conflicts. This subchapter aims to provide practical strategies and insights on how to improve your communication skills through active listening and empathy.

Active listening is a skill that involves fully engaging with the speaker and understanding their perspective. It goes beyond simply hearing the words being spoken. When you actively listen, you make a conscious effort to give your undivided attention and show genuine interest in what the speaker is saying. This means maintaining eye contact, nodding or providing verbal cues to indicate understanding, and refraining from interrupting or making assumptions.

Empathy, on the other hand, is the ability to understand and share the feelings of another person. It involves putting yourself in their shoes and seeing the world from their perspective. Empathy allows you to connect with others on a deeper level, fostering trust and creating a safe space for open and honest communication.

So how can you develop these skills and apply them in your daily interactions? Firstly, practice active listening by eliminating distractions and focusing solely on the speaker. Avoid multitasking and give your full attention to the conversation at hand. Secondly, show empathy by acknowledging and validating the speaker's emotions. Reflect back on what they are saying and try to understand the underlying feelings behind their words.

Another effective technique is to ask open-ended questions to encourage the speaker to share more details and express their thoughts and emotions. This not only shows that you are actively listening but also allows the speaker to delve deeper into their own understanding of the situation.

Moreover, be aware of nonverbal cues such as body language and tone of voice. These subtle signs can provide valuable insights into the speaker's emotions and help you respond appropriately. By paying attention to these cues, you demonstrate your empathy and show that you genuinely care about the speaker's experience.

By practicing active listening and empathy, you can break down barriers to effective communication and build stronger connections with others. These skills are not limited to the workplace but can be applied in all areas of life. Whether it is resolving conflicts, building relationships, or simply improving your day-to-day interactions, active listening and empathy are essential tools for better communication. Start implementing these strategies today and witness the positive impact they can have on your personal and professional life.

Effective Verbal and Nonverbal Communication

Communication is an essential aspect of human interaction, influencing our relationships, work environments, and overall quality of life. Whether you are communicating with a colleague, a loved one, or even a stranger, mastering the art of effective verbal and nonverbal communication can greatly enhance your ability to connect, understand, and resolve conflicts.

Verbal communication encompasses the words we choose, the tone of our voice, and the clarity of our message. It is crucial to express ourselves clearly and concisely, ensuring that our words accurately convey our intentions. Using simple and direct language helps to eliminate misunderstandings and confusion. Additionally, paying attention to our tone of voice can greatly impact how our message is received. Speaking in a calm, respectful, and confident manner fosters a positive atmosphere and promotes effective communication.

Nonverbal communication, often referred to as body language, plays an equally important role in conveying our thoughts and feelings. Our facial expressions, gestures, posture, and even eye contact can speak volumes about our emotions and intentions. For instance, maintaining good eye contact shows attentiveness and interest, while crossed arms may indicate defensiveness or disengagement. By being aware of and controlling our nonverbal cues, we can better align our message with our body language, fostering trust and understanding.

In the workplace, effective verbal and nonverbal communication is particularly crucial. It facilitates collaboration, reduces misunderstandings, and enhances productivity. By actively listening to our colleagues, we not only demonstrate respect but also gain valuable insights and information. Furthermore, being mindful of our nonverbal cues helps us to build rapport and establish positive connections with our coworkers.

Beyond the workplace, effective communication is equally important in personal relationships. By being attentive and present during conversations, we show our loved ones that we value and respect their thoughts and feelings. Open and honest communication fosters trust, intimacy, and mutual understanding.

In conclusion, mastering effective verbal and nonverbal communication is vital for everyone. By honing these skills, we can break down barriers, resolve conflicts, and build stronger relationships. Whether in the workplace or in our personal lives, effective communication empowers us to express ourselves, understand others, and navigate through life with confidence and success.

Collaborative Problem-Solving

In our modern world, effective problem-solving is a crucial skill that can make a significant difference in both personal and professional relationships. When conflicts arise, it is essential to approach them with a collaborative mindset, seeking solutions that benefit all parties involved. This subchapter will explore the concept of collaborative problem-solving, providing practical strategies for resolving conflicts and improving communication.

Collaborative problem-solving is a process that involves a group of individuals working together to find a mutually agreeable solution. It requires active listening, empathy, and open-mindedness. By pooling resources and ideas, collaborative problem-solving enables individuals to tap into the collective wisdom of a group, leading to more innovative and sustainable solutions.

One of the key components of collaborative problem-solving is effective communication. By fostering an environment where everyone feels heard and respected, conflicts can be resolved more efficiently. Active listening is a crucial skill, as it allows individuals to fully understand the perspectives and concerns of others. By putting ourselves in each other's shoes, we can gain empathy and build bridges of understanding.

To engage in collaborative problem-solving, it is important to focus on common goals rather than personal agendas. By shifting the focus to finding a mutually beneficial solution, individuals can work together towards a shared objective. This approach fosters a sense of teamwork and cultivates trust among team members.

Furthermore, collaborative problem-solving requires a willingness to brainstorm and explore various options. Encouraging creativity and diversity of ideas allows for a wider range of solutions to be considered. Engaging in constructive dialogue and respectful debate can lead to breakthroughs and innovative problem-solving approaches.

However, it is essential to remember that collaborative problem-solving does not always guarantee immediate resolution. Some conflicts may require time, patience, and compromise. It is important to be flexible and willing to adapt one's position for the greater good.

By embracing collaborative problem-solving, we can break down barriers that hinder effective communication and conflict resolution. This approach not only strengthens relationships but also promotes a culture of cooperation and collaboration. Whether in the workplace or in personal relationships, the ability to collaboratively solve problems is a valuable skill that benefits everyone involved.

In conclusion, collaborative problem-solving is a powerful tool for resolving conflicts and improving communication. By fostering a culture of active listening, empathy, and open-mindedness, individuals can work together towards finding solutions that benefit all parties involved. Through effective communication, a focus on common goals, and a willingness to explore various options, collaborative problem-solving can lead to breakthroughs and stronger relationships. By embracing this approach, we can break barriers and achieve effective conflict resolution in both personal and professional settings.

Negotiation and Compromise

Negotiation and Compromise: Building Bridges for Effective Communication

In our daily lives, conflicts and disagreements are inevitable. Whether it is in the workplace, at home, or in our relationships, differing opinions and interests can often lead to tension and misunderstandings. However, learning the art of negotiation and compromise can be the key to resolving conflicts and fostering effective communication. In this subchapter, we will explore strategies for breaking barriers and finding common ground through negotiation and compromise.

Negotiation is a process of reaching an agreement by discussing and exploring options that satisfy the needs and interests of all parties involved. It requires active listening, empathy, and a willingness to find mutually beneficial solutions. By engaging in negotiation, we can bridge the gap between different perspectives and foster understanding.

Compromise, on the other hand, involves finding a middle ground where both parties give up something in order to reach a solution. It requires flexibility, open-mindedness, and a focus on the bigger picture. Compromise is not about winning or losing; it is about finding a fair and reasonable resolution that respects the needs and concerns of all parties.

To negotiate and compromise effectively, it is essential to cultivate effective communication skills. Active listening allows us to understand the underlying interests and concerns of others. By acknowledging and validating these concerns, we create an environment of trust and respect. This paves the way for productive discussions where all parties feel heard and understood.

Additionally, effective communication involves expressing our own needs and interests clearly and assertively. By using "I" statements and avoiding accusatory language, we can convey our perspective without provoking defensiveness or hostility. This encourages a collaborative atmosphere where everyone's ideas are valued.

In negotiation and compromise, it is crucial to focus on common goals and shared interests. By shifting the focus from positions to interests, we can identify creative solutions that satisfy everyone involved. This requires thinking outside the box and exploring alternative options that meet the underlying needs of each party.

Finally, negotiation and compromise require patience and a willingness to explore different possibilities. It is important to remember that reaching an agreement may take time and multiple iterations. By maintaining a positive attitude and staying committed to finding a resolution, we can break barriers and build bridges for effective communication.

In conclusion, negotiation and compromise are essential tools for resolving conflicts and fostering effective communication. By cultivating active listening, expressing our needs assertively, and focusing on common goals, we can find mutually beneficial solutions that satisfy all parties involved. In doing so, we bridge the gap between different perspectives and create an atmosphere of understanding and collaboration. Regardless of our roles or backgrounds, mastering the art of negotiation and compromise is a valuable skill that can benefit everyone in all aspects of life.

Chapter 4: Building Effective Communication Skills

Clear and Concise Communication

In today's fast-paced world, effective communication is more important than ever. Whether you are communicating at work or in your personal life, being able to convey your message clearly and concisely is crucial. This subchapter, titled "Clear and Concise Communication," explores the strategies and techniques that can help you improve your communication skills and break down barriers.

Communication is the key to successful relationships, both professional and personal. However, it can often be challenging to express ourselves in a way that is easily understood by others. This subchapter aims to provide you with the tools you need to communicate better, both at work and beyond.

The first step to clear and concise communication is to know your audience. Understanding who you are speaking to will help you tailor your message to their needs and interests. This subchapter will guide you on how to identify your audience and adjust your communication style accordingly.

In addition to knowing your audience, it is essential to be aware of your own communication style. Are you speaking too quickly? Are you using jargon that others might not understand? This subchapter will help you analyze your communication style and provide tips on how to make it more clear and concise.

Furthermore, this subchapter will delve into the importance of active listening. Effective communication is a two-way street, and being able to listen actively is just as crucial as speaking clearly. You will learn techniques to improve your listening skills, such as paraphrasing and asking clarifying questions.

Moreover, this subchapter will explore the power of non-verbal communication. Our body language, facial expressions, and tone of voice can often convey more than our words. Understanding how to use non-verbal cues effectively will enhance your ability to communicate clearly and concisely.

Finally, this subchapter will discuss the role of technology in communication and how to navigate its challenges. With the rise of email, texting, and video conferencing, it is essential to adapt your communication skills to these platforms. You will learn how to write effective emails, give clear instructions over the phone, and present confidently in virtual meetings.

In conclusion, clear and concise communication is a skill that everyone can benefit from. Whether you are communicating at work or in your personal life, these strategies and techniques will help you break down barriers and improve your relationships. By understanding your audience, adjusting your communication style, actively listening, utilizing non-verbal cues, and adapting to technology, you will become a more effective communicator in all areas of your life.

Assertiveness and Conflict Management

In today's fast-paced and interconnected world, effective communication and conflict resolution skills have become more crucial than ever. Whether you are interacting with colleagues at work, navigating personal relationships, or simply engaging with others in your day-to-day life, the ability to assertively express your needs and manage conflicts can greatly enhance your overall well-being and success.

This subchapter, titled "Assertiveness and Conflict Management," delves into the key strategies and techniques that can help you navigate through challenging situations and communicate better with others. Drawing from the book "Breaking Barriers: Strategies for Conflict Resolution and Effective Communication," this content is designed to cater to a diverse audience, including individuals seeking to improve their communication skills at work and beyond.

Assertiveness is a fundamental component of effective communication. It involves expressing your thoughts, feelings, and needs in a clear and respectful manner, without infringing upon the rights of others. This subchapter explores the importance of assertiveness and provides practical tools to help you develop this essential skill. From understanding the difference between assertiveness and aggression to learning how to use "I" statements effectively, you will gain valuable insights into assertive communication.

Conflict is an inevitable part of life, but how we manage it can make all the difference. This subchapter delves into various conflict management strategies that can help you navigate through disagreements and find mutually beneficial resolutions. You will learn about different conflict resolution styles, such as collaboration, compromise, and avoidance, and gain a deeper understanding of when to employ each approach.

Furthermore, this subchapter recognizes the significance of effective communication in conflict management. It explores active listening techniques, empathy-building strategies, and the art of asking open-ended questions to foster understanding and find common ground.

By mastering assertiveness and conflict management, you will not only enhance your personal relationships but also excel in the workplace. This subchapter provides real-life examples, case studies, and practical exercises to help you apply these strategies in various scenarios.

Whether you are a manager seeking to improve team dynamics or an individual striving for personal growth, the content within this subchapter will empower you to communicate better, resolve conflicts effectively, and ultimately break barriers in your interpersonal relationships.

"Assertiveness and Conflict Management" is a subchapter within the book "Breaking Barriers: Strategies for Conflict Resolution and Effective Communication." It is a valuable resource for everyone seeking to improve their communication skills, from professionals looking to excel in the workplace to individuals aiming to build healthier and more fulfilling relationships. By incorporating the principles and techniques outlined in this subchapter, you will be better equipped to navigate conflicts, assert your needs, and communicate more effectively in all facets of life.

Emotional Intelligence

In today's fast-paced world, effective communication and conflict resolution have become essential skills for everyone. To truly excel in these areas, it is crucial to develop emotional intelligence. Emotional intelligence is the ability to recognize, understand, and manage our own emotions, as well as the emotions of others. It acts as a guiding compass in navigating the complex landscape of human interactions and plays a vital role in achieving success, both in our personal and professional lives.

At its core, emotional intelligence allows us to build stronger relationships, foster empathy, and improve communication. By being aware of our own emotions, we can better understand how they influence our thoughts and behaviors. This self-awareness enables us to regulate our emotions effectively, preventing impulsive reactions and allowing us to respond in a more rational and constructive manner. Additionally, emotional intelligence helps us develop empathy towards others, as we can recognize and appreciate their emotions.

In the workplace, emotional intelligence is a valuable asset. It allows us to communicate better with colleagues, superiors, and subordinates, fostering a positive work environment and facilitating collaboration. Through emotional intelligence, we can better understand the needs and concerns of others, leading to more effective conflict resolution. By managing our emotions and responding empathetically, we can de-escalate tense situations and find mutually beneficial solutions.

Beyond the workplace, emotional intelligence plays a critical role in our personal relationships. By understanding and managing our own emotions, we can communicate our feelings more effectively, leading to healthier and more fulfilling connections. Similarly, by recognizing the emotions of our loved ones, we can deepen our understanding and offer support when needed. Emotional intelligence allows us to build trust, foster intimacy, and navigate conflicts constructively, ultimately strengthening our bonds.

To develop emotional intelligence, it is important to engage in self-reflection, actively listening to our emotions and examining their impact on our thoughts and actions. Practicing empathy and seeking to understand the emotions of others also helps us strengthen this skill. By becoming more aware of our own emotions and those of others, we can enhance our ability to communicate, resolve conflicts, and build meaningful relationships.

In conclusion, emotional intelligence is a vital skill for everyone, regardless of their professional or personal background. By cultivating emotional intelligence, we can communicate better at work and beyond, breaking barriers and paving the way for effective conflict resolution. Developing this skill empowers us to build stronger relationships, foster empathy, and navigate the complexities of human interactions with grace and understanding.

Nonviolent Communication

Nonviolent Communication: Building Bridges for Effective Communication

In a world filled with conflicts and misunderstandings, the need for effective communication has never been greater. In the subchapter of "Breaking Barriers: Strategies for Conflict Resolution and Effective Communication" titled "Nonviolent Communication," we explore a powerful approach that can transform how we connect with others, both at work and beyond. This approach, known as Nonviolent Communication (NVC), offers a framework for fostering empathy, understanding, and peaceful resolution of conflicts.

NVC, developed by Marshall B. Rosenberg, is based on the idea that all human beings have the capacity for compassion and empathy. It aims to create a bridge between individuals by encouraging open and honest dialogue while fostering a deep understanding of each other's needs. By focusing on four key components – observations, feelings, needs, and requests – NVC provides a roadmap for building connections and resolving conflicts without resorting to violence or aggression.

In the workplace, effective communication is vital for productivity, teamwork, and overall success. By incorporating NVC principles, employees can create a harmonious work environment where everyone feels heard and valued. By listening with empathy, expressing oneself honestly but non-judgmentally, and seeking to understand the underlying needs and motivations of others, conflicts can be transformed into opportunities for growth and collaboration.

Beyond the workplace, Nonviolent Communication can enhance our personal relationships, enabling us to communicate more authentically and compassionately. By recognizing and expressing our feelings and needs, we can avoid misunderstandings, build trust, and create deeper connections with our loved ones. NVC also encourages us to understand the feelings and needs of others, fostering empathy and promoting understanding even in difficult or challenging situations.

Nonviolent Communication is not just a set of techniques; it's a mindset and a way of being. By cultivating empathy, understanding, and compassion, we can break down barriers and create a more peaceful and harmonious world. Whether you're a professional seeking better communication at work or an individual looking to improve your personal relationships, the principles of Nonviolent Communication can benefit everyone.

In the forthcoming chapters of "Breaking Barriers: Strategies for Conflict Resolution and Effective Communication," we will delve deeper into the practical application of NVC, providing real-life examples, strategies, and exercises to help you integrate this powerful approach into your daily life. So, join us on this journey of discovery and transformation as we explore the art of Nonviolent Communication and unlock the true power of effective communication.

Chapter 5: Overcoming Barriers to Communication

Cultural and Language Differences

In our globalized world, it is becoming increasingly important to understand and navigate the cultural and language differences that exist among us. Whether it is in the workplace, in our personal relationships, or even while traveling, being aware of these differences is essential for effective communication and conflict resolution. This subchapter aims to provide insights and strategies to help everyone improve their understanding and bridge the gaps caused by cultural and language barriers.

Cultural differences can manifest in various ways, including norms, values, customs, and traditions. Understanding and appreciating these differences is crucial for building strong relationships and avoiding misunderstandings. By recognizing that people from different cultures may have distinct communication styles, expectations, and even personal space boundaries, we can adapt our own behavior and communication approach accordingly. This willingness to adapt and be open-minded fosters a more inclusive and respectful environment.

Language barriers can also pose challenges when trying to communicate effectively. Misunderstandings can easily arise due to different interpretations of words, phrases, or gestures. It is important to approach conversations with patience and empathy, especially when communicating with non-native speakers. Simplifying language, using clear and concise sentences, and avoiding idioms or jargon can greatly enhance understanding and avoid confusion.

To overcome cultural and language differences, active listening is paramount. Taking the time to listen and understand others' perspectives, without judgment, allows for a more meaningful exchange of ideas. It is also essential to ask clarifying questions when needed, rather than making assumptions or jumping to conclusions based on our own cultural biases.

In addition, educating ourselves about different cultures and languages is an ongoing process. Reading books, attending cultural events, or even taking language classes can significantly enhance our ability to communicate effectively and respectfully across cultures. By demonstrating a genuine interest in others' cultures and languages, we promote understanding and build stronger connections.

In conclusion, cultural and language differences are a natural part of our diverse world. By acknowledging and embracing these differences, we can foster better communication and conflict resolution in all areas of our lives. By continuously learning and adapting our communication styles, we can break down barriers and build bridges that allow us to connect with others on a deeper level.

Misinterpretation and Assumptions

In our day-to-day interactions, misinterpretation and assumptions often pose significant barriers to effective communication. Whether at work or in personal relationships, these misunderstandings can lead to conflicts, strained relationships, and missed opportunities. Recognizing and addressing these challenges is crucial for anyone seeking to improve their communication skills and resolve conflicts.

One common pitfall is the tendency to assume that others share our perspective or understand things in the same way we do. We often make assumptions about people's intentions, beliefs, or motivations without seeking clarification. These assumptions can result in misunderstandings and miscommunication.

To overcome this barrier, it is essential to practice active listening and engage in open dialogue. Active listening involves giving our full attention to the speaker, seeking clarification when necessary, and avoiding making assumptions. By asking questions and paraphrasing what the speaker has said, we can ensure that we have correctly understood their message.

Another aspect of misinterpretation comes from differences in cultural or personal backgrounds. Our own experiences and beliefs shape how we interpret and understand the world around us. When communicating with individuals from diverse backgrounds, it is crucial to be aware of these differences and approach conversations with empathy and an open mind.

Breaking down misinterpretations and assumptions requires effective communication strategies. One such strategy is to use clear and concise language. Avoid using jargon or technical terms when speaking to someone who may not be familiar with them. Instead, aim for simplicity and clarity to ensure your message is understood as intended.

Non-verbal communication also plays a significant role in avoiding misinterpretations. Body language, facial expressions, and tone of voice can convey messages that are complementary or contradictory to our spoken words. Being mindful of our non-verbal cues and observing those of others can help us better understand the underlying message and avoid misunderstandings.

Finally, it is crucial to approach communication with a growth mindset. Instead of assuming that conflicts are unsolvable or that misunderstandings are inevitable, we should view them as opportunities for growth and learning. By embracing a mindset of curiosity and a willingness to understand different perspectives, we can break down barriers and foster effective communication.

In conclusion, misinterpretation and assumptions are common hurdles in communication that can lead to conflicts and strained relationships. By actively listening, being aware of cultural differences, using clear language, paying attention to non-verbal cues, and adopting a growth mindset, we can overcome these barriers and communicate effectively. These strategies are essential for everyone, both in the workplace and in personal interactions, as they promote better understanding, empathy, and collaboration. By breaking down these barriers, we can build stronger connections and resolve conflicts more effectively.

Emotional Barriers

In our journey towards effective communication and conflict resolution, it is crucial to address the emotional barriers that can hinder our progress. Emotions play a significant role in our interactions with others, and if not managed properly, they can lead to misunderstandings, conflicts, and a breakdown in communication. In this subchapter, we will delve into the concept of emotional barriers and explore strategies to overcome them.

Emotional barriers are hurdles that prevent us from expressing ourselves clearly and listening to others with empathy. These barriers can manifest in various ways, such as fear, anger, anxiety, or even past experiences that have shaped our emotional responses. Understanding and managing these barriers is essential for enhancing our communication skills and fostering healthier relationships, both at work and beyond.

One common emotional barrier is fear. Fear of judgment, rejection, or confrontation can inhibit our ability to express our thoughts and feelings openly. By acknowledging and addressing this fear, we can begin to build trust and create a safe environment where open communication can flourish. Techniques such as deep breathing, positive self-talk, and visualization can help alleviate fear and allow us to communicate more confidently.

Anger is another emotional barrier that can hinder effective communication. When we are angry, our judgment becomes clouded, and rational thinking takes a backseat. It is crucial to recognize the signs of anger and take steps to calm ourselves before engaging in any communication. Techniques like counting to ten, taking a break, or practicing mindfulness can help us regain control over our emotions and respond more constructively.

Past experiences can also create emotional barriers. Negative experiences, such as previous conflicts or betrayals, can make us wary of opening up and trusting others. It is vital to acknowledge these past experiences, but not let them dictate our present interactions. By practicing forgiveness, empathy, and giving others the benefit of the doubt, we can gradually break down these emotional barriers and foster healthier connections.

In conclusion, emotional barriers can impede effective communication and conflict resolution. By identifying and addressing our fears, managing anger, and overcoming past experiences, we can break through these barriers and communicate better at work and beyond. It is essential to remember that everyone faces emotional barriers to some extent, and we must approach communication with empathy and understanding. By doing so, we can create an atmosphere of trust, respect, and open dialogue, leading to more successful conflict resolution and improved relationships.

External Factors: Noise, Distractions, and Technology

In today's fast-paced world, effective communication has become a crucial skill for success in both personal and professional settings. However, there are numerous external factors that can hinder our ability to communicate effectively. This subchapter explores the impact of noise, distractions, and technology on communication and provides strategies to overcome these obstacles.

Noise is one of the most common external factors that can disrupt communication. Whether it's the loud chatter of coworkers in an open office or the constant hum of traffic outside, excessive noise can make it difficult to concentrate and convey our thoughts clearly. To overcome this challenge, it is important to find quiet places or create a designated space where communication can take place without distractions. Additionally, using tools like noise-canceling headphones or white noise machines can help minimize the impact of ambient noise.

Distractions, both internal and external, can also impede effective communication. Internal distractions such as personal thoughts and emotions can divert our attention from the conversation at hand. It is crucial to practice mindfulness and actively listen to others, setting aside personal distractions to fully engage in the communication process. External distractions, on the other hand, can be more challenging to avoid. In today's digital age, smartphones, social media, and constant notifications compete for our attention. To combat this, it is important to establish boundaries and set aside dedicated time for communication without the interference of technology.

Speaking of technology, while it has undoubtedly revolutionized communication, it can also be a double-edged sword. While it allows us to connect with others across vast distances, it can also create barriers to effective communication. Misinterpretation of messages, lack of non-verbal cues, and the ease of multitasking can all hinder the clarity and depth of our communication. To mitigate these challenges, it is important to be mindful of our technology usage. When engaged in important conversations, it is best to put away distractions and focus on the present moment.

In conclusion, external factors such as noise, distractions, and technology present significant challenges to effective communication. By understanding and addressing these obstacles, we can enhance our communication skills and forge stronger connections with others. By creating conducive environments, minimizing distractions, and being mindful of technology usage, we can break the barriers that hinder effective communication, both at work and in our personal lives. Remember, effective communication is a lifelong skill that can be honed with practice and patience, leading to better relationships, increased understanding, and overall success in all aspects of life.

Chapter 6: Conflict Resolution in Personal Relationships

Communication Styles in Relationships

Effective communication is the cornerstone of successful relationships, whether they are personal or professional. In the book "Breaking Barriers: Strategies for Conflict Resolution and Effective Communication," we delve into the various communication styles that can significantly impact relationships. Understanding these styles can help individuals navigate conflicts, foster understanding, and build stronger connections with others.

When it comes to communication styles in relationships, it is essential to recognize that everyone has their unique way of expressing themselves. Some individuals may be more assertive, while others are more passive or even passive-aggressive. By understanding these styles, we can adapt our own approach to communication and better understand others' perspectives.

Assertive communication is often considered the most effective style in relationships. It involves expressing one's thoughts, feelings, and needs while respecting others' rights and boundaries. Individuals who utilize assertive communication are honest, direct, and confident in expressing themselves. They actively listen to others, seeking to understand them rather than simply responding. This style encourages open and honest dialogue, fostering trust and respect in relationships.

Passive communication, on the other hand, involves avoiding conflict or confrontation altogether. Individuals who use this style tend to prioritize the needs of others over their own, often leading to frustration and unmet expectations. Passive communicators may struggle to express their true thoughts and feelings, leading to misunderstandings and resentment within relationships.

Passive-aggressive communication combines elements of both passive and aggressive styles. Individuals using this style might express their anger or frustration indirectly, often through sarcasm, subtle digs, or passive behavior. This approach often leads to a cycle of miscommunication and escalating conflicts, as the underlying issues are not addressed directly.

By understanding these communication styles, we can recognize our own tendencies and how they impact our relationships. Moreover, we can learn to adapt our style to better connect with others. Developing assertive communication skills can help individuals express their needs clearly and honestly while acknowledging and respecting the perspectives of others.

In conclusion, effective communication is vital in all relationships, and understanding the different communication styles can significantly improve our interactions. By recognizing and adapting our own style, we can foster open and honest dialogue, resolve conflicts, and build stronger connections. The book "Breaking Barriers: Strategies for Conflict Resolution and Effective Communication" offers further insights into effective communication techniques, empowering everyone to communicate better at work and beyond.

Managing Conflict in Romantic Relationships

Conflict is an inevitable part of any relationship, including romantic ones. When two individuals with different backgrounds, values, and perspectives come together, disagreements are bound to arise. However, conflict does not have to be detrimental to a relationship. In fact, when managed effectively, conflict can serve as a catalyst for personal growth, deeper understanding, and stronger bonds. This subchapter will delve into strategies for managing conflict in romantic relationships, offering insights and practical advice for individuals seeking to navigate these challenges.

The Importance of Effective Communication:

At the heart of managing conflict lies effective communication. Open and honest dialogue allows partners to express their needs, concerns, and emotions without fear of judgment or retaliation. It is essential to create a safe and non-threatening environment where both individuals feel comfortable expressing themselves. Active listening, empathy, and validation play crucial roles in fostering effective communication.

Identifying and Addressing Core Issues:

Conflict often arises from underlying issues that may not be immediately apparent. It is important to identify these core issues and address them directly rather than focusing solely on the surface-level problem. By digging deeper, partners can gain a better understanding of each other's needs and motivations, leading to more meaningful resolutions.

Finding Common Ground:

During conflicts, it is easy to become entrenched in one's own perspective, leading to a stalemate. Finding common ground can break this deadlock and allow partners to work towards a mutually beneficial solution. It involves exploring shared values, goals, and interests, and finding compromises that honor both individuals' needs.

Managing Emotions and Avoiding Escalation:

Emotions often run high during conflicts, making it challenging to have productive conversations. Learning to manage emotions and avoiding escalation is crucial in resolving conflicts effectively. Techniques such as taking breaks, practicing self-soothing, and using "I" statements can help partners de-escalate tense situations and approach conflicts with a level head.

Seeking Professional Help:

In some cases, conflicts may become too complex or deeply rooted for partners to handle alone. Seeking the assistance of a trained professional, such as a couples therapist, can provide invaluable guidance and support. Therapists can help couples navigate conflicts, develop healthier communication patterns, and work towards a more fulfilling relationship.

Conclusion:

Conflict is a natural part of romantic relationships, but it does not have to be detrimental. By fostering effective communication, addressing core issues, finding common ground, managing emotions, and seeking professional help when needed, couples can navigate conflicts with greater ease and strengthen their relationship in the process. Remember, conflict is an opportunity for growth and deeper connection, as long as it is managed with care, respect, and understanding.

Resolving Conflict within Families

In a world filled with diverse opinions, values, and personalities, conflicts within families are an inevitable part of life. However, navigating these conflicts with grace and understanding can lead to stronger and more harmonious family relationships. In this subchapter, we will explore effective strategies for resolving conflicts within families, promoting open communication, and fostering a peaceful environment at home.

First and foremost, it is crucial to acknowledge that conflicts are a natural part of human relationships. Rather than avoiding or suppressing conflicts, we should embrace them as opportunities for growth and understanding. Conflict resolution begins with active listening, where each family member takes the time to genuinely hear and understand the perspective of others. By showing empathy and respect, we can create an environment where everyone feels comfortable expressing their thoughts and emotions.

Another important aspect of resolving family conflicts is finding common ground. Often, conflicts arise from misunderstandings or differences in values and beliefs. By focusing on shared interests and goals, family members can find areas of agreement and build upon them. This approach helps shift the focus from individual differences to collective solutions, leading to more effective problem-solving.

Furthermore, effective communication is key to resolving conflicts within families. It is essential to choose words carefully, avoiding blame or criticism, and instead expressing feelings and needs in a respectful manner. Additionally, non-verbal cues such as body language and tone of voice can greatly impact the outcome of a conversation. By maintaining an open and non-judgmental stance, family members can create an environment conducive to constructive dialogue.

Conflict resolution within families also requires compromise and negotiation. It is essential to recognize that no one person's needs or desires should dominate the family dynamic. Instead, family members should strive for mutual understanding and find solutions that accommodate everyone's interests. This may involve brainstorming creative alternatives or seeking outside help such as family therapy or counseling.

Lastly, forgiveness and reconciliation play a vital role in resolving conflicts within families. Holding onto grudges or unresolved issues can create resentment and further division. By practicing forgiveness and seeking reconciliation, family members can heal emotional wounds and rebuild trust, strengthening the family bond.

In conclusion, conflicts within families are a natural part of life, but they can be resolved effectively through open communication, active listening, finding common ground, compromise, and forgiveness. By implementing these strategies, families can overcome conflicts and build stronger, more harmonious relationships. Remember, resolving conflicts takes time and effort, but the rewards of a peaceful and loving family environment are truly priceless.

Conflict Resolution in Friendships

Friendships are an essential part of our lives, providing us with companionship, support, and shared experiences. However, like any relationship, conflicts can arise in friendships, leading to tension and misunderstandings. In this subchapter, we will explore effective strategies for conflict resolution in friendships, helping you navigate these challenges and foster healthier, more fulfilling connections.

1. Communication is Key: Open and honest communication lies at the heart of resolving conflicts in friendships. When conflicts arise, it is crucial to express your thoughts and emotions in a calm and respectful manner. Actively listen to your friend's perspective, allowing them to share their feelings and concerns without interruption. By creating a safe space for open dialogue, you can gain a better understanding of each other's needs and work towards finding common ground.

2. Seek Understanding: Conflict often arises from misunderstandings or miscommunication. Take the time to understand your friend's point of view, asking clarifying questions and empathizing with their emotions. Avoid making assumptions or jumping to conclusions, as this can exacerbate the conflict. By actively seeking understanding, you create an environment of empathy and compassion, paving the way for resolution.

3. Find a Win-Win Solution: When conflicts arise, it is easy to fall into a win-lose mindset, where one person's needs are prioritized over the other. However, in friendships, it is important to find a win-win solution that addresses the concerns of both parties. Brainstorm creative alternatives and compromises that can satisfy both sides. Remember, friendship is built on mutual respect and fairness.

4. Apologize and Forgive: In any conflict, it is often necessary for both parties to take responsibility for their actions. If you have made a mistake, apologize sincerely and take steps to rectify the situation. Equally important is the ability to forgive. Holding onto grudges and resentment can strain friendships and hinder resolution. Practice forgiveness, allowing for growth and healing in your relationship.

5. Seek Mediation if Needed: In some cases, conflicts in friendships may escalate to a point where external intervention is necessary. If you and your friend are unable to resolve the conflict on your own, consider

seeking the help of a neutral third party, such as a trusted mutual friend or a professional mediator. Their objective perspective can facilitate productive discussions and guide you toward resolution.

In conclusion, conflicts are a natural part of friendships, but they can be resolved through effective communication, understanding, compromise, and forgiveness. By employing these strategies, you can break down barriers, strengthen your friendships, and create a harmonious and supportive network. Remember, conflict resolution in friendships requires effort and commitment from both parties, but the rewards are immeasurable – deeper connections, personal growth, and lifelong companionship.

Chapter 7: Conflict Resolution in the Workplace

Effective Communication in the Workplace

Communication is the cornerstone of any successful organization. It is the lifeblood that keeps teams connected, fosters collaboration, and drives productivity. In the fast-paced world we live in, the ability to communicate effectively has become more important than ever. Whether you are a manager, employee, or team member, mastering the art of communication is crucial in order to excel in the workplace.

This chapter of "Breaking Barriers: Strategies for Conflict Resolution and Effective Communication" aims to provide practical insights and strategies to help everyone enhance their communication skills. By understanding the power of effective communication, individuals can build stronger relationships, resolve conflicts, and achieve their professional goals.

Within the workplace, effective communication plays a vital role in various aspects of daily operations. Clear and concise communication helps in conveying ideas, instructions, and expectations accurately. It reduces misunderstandings, prevents conflicts, and enhances teamwork. Moreover, effective communication also creates a positive work environment, fostering trust, respect, and engagement among employees.

To communicate better at work and beyond, it is essential to develop active listening skills. Listening attentively not only helps in understanding the message being conveyed, but it also shows respect and empathy towards the speaker. Additionally, effective communication involves choosing the right medium for conveying your message. Whether it's face-to-face conversations, emails, or digital platforms, understanding the strengths and limitations of each medium is crucial for effective communication.

In this subchapter, we will also explore the importance of non-verbal communication. Body language, facial expressions, and tone of voice can often convey more than words alone. Developing an awareness of non-verbal cues can significantly improve your ability to understand others and express yourself more effectively.

Furthermore, effective communication requires the ability to adapt your message to different audiences. Understanding the needs, perspectives, and communication styles of others enables you to tailor your approach and ensure your message is received and understood.

By implementing the strategies and insights provided in this subchapter, readers will be equipped with the tools to communicate more effectively in the workplace and beyond. Improved communication skills will not only enhance professional relationships but also contribute to personal growth and success. Whether you are a seasoned professional or just starting your career, mastering the art of effective communication is a lifelong journey that will undoubtedly open doors to endless opportunities.

Conflict Resolution Strategies for Teams and Groups

In today's fast-paced world, working in teams and groups is inevitable. Whether you are part of a small team or a large group, conflicts are bound to arise. However, conflicts should not be seen as negative experiences; they can actually be opportunities for growth and learning if handled effectively. This subchapter will explore various conflict resolution strategies that can be applied to teams and groups, helping individuals communicate better at work and beyond.

1. Active Listening: One of the most effective conflict resolution strategies is active listening. Encourage team members to truly listen to each other's perspectives without interrupting or judging. This fosters empathy and understanding, allowing for better communication and resolution.

2. Collaborative Problem Solving: Instead of approaching conflicts as a win-lose situation, promote a collaborative problem-solving approach. Encourage the team or group to work together to find mutually beneficial solutions. This approach ensures that everyone's needs and interests are considered, resulting in more sustainable resolutions.

3. Clear Communication: Effective communication is crucial in resolving conflicts. Encourage team members to express their thoughts and concerns clearly and respectfully. Emphasize the importance of using "I" statements to avoid blaming or accusing others, keeping the focus on the issue at hand.

4. Mediation and Facilitation: Sometimes conflicts may require the intervention of a neutral third party. Introduce the concept of mediation and facilitation, where a trained individual helps guide the resolution process. This can be particularly useful in situations where emotions are running high or when there is a power imbalance within the team or group.

5. Building Trust and Respect: Conflict resolution is much easier in an environment where trust and respect exist. Encourage team members to build positive relationships by recognizing and appreciating each other's strengths and contributions. Foster an inclusive and supportive atmosphere where everyone feels valued and heard.

6. Learning from Conflict: Conflict resolution should not be seen as the end goal but rather as a means of growth and improvement. Encourage individuals to reflect on conflict situations and identify lessons learned. This allows teams and groups to develop better strategies for preventing and managing conflicts in the future.

In conclusion, conflict resolution strategies are essential for effective communication and collaboration within teams and groups. By promoting active listening, collaborative problem-solving, clear communication, mediation and facilitation, trust and respect, and learning from conflict, individuals can navigate conflicts more successfully. These strategies are applicable in various settings, from the workplace to personal relationships, making them valuable tools for everyone.

Handling Difficult Colleagues or Bosses

In any workplace, dealing with difficult colleagues or bosses can be a challenging task. However, effective communication and conflict resolution strategies can help navigate these sticky situations, allowing you to maintain a harmonious work environment. This subchapter aims to equip everyone with the necessary tools to handle difficult colleagues or bosses, ensuring better communication at work and beyond.

Recognizing the signs of difficult colleagues or bosses is the first step toward finding a resolution. They may exhibit traits such as aggression, micromanagement, or a lack of respect for others' opinions. Understanding these behaviors can help you adopt the appropriate approach in dealing with them.

One of the essential strategies for handling difficult colleagues or bosses is active listening. By giving them your full attention and acknowledging their concerns, you can establish a foundation for effective communication. It is crucial to stay calm and composed, even in the face of adversity, as reacting impulsively may escalate the situation further.

Another vital technique is assertive communication. Expressing your thoughts and feelings in a clear, respectful, and confident manner can help diffuse tension and foster understanding. By using "I" statements and focusing on specific behaviors rather than attacking the person, you can convey your concerns without causing defensiveness or hostility.

When conflicts arise, it is essential to address them promptly. Ignoring or avoiding the issue will only exacerbate the problem. Instead, initiate open and honest conversations, seeking common ground and potential solutions. By approaching the situation with empathy and understanding, you can work towards a mutually beneficial resolution.

Furthermore, building positive relationships can help mitigate conflicts in the workplace. By fostering a supportive and collaborative environment, you can reduce the likelihood of difficult situations arising. Engaging in team-building activities, providing constructive feedback, and promoting a culture of respect and inclusivity can contribute to a more harmonious work environment.

Lastly, self-care is crucial when dealing with difficult colleagues or bosses. Recognize your limits and take the necessary steps to protect your well-being. Seek support from trusted friends, family, or mentors, and consider seeking professional help if the situation becomes overwhelming.

In conclusion, handling difficult colleagues or bosses requires effective communication, conflict resolution strategies, and a mindful approach. By adopting active listening, assertive communication, and addressing conflicts promptly, you can foster a positive work environment that encourages open dialogue and collaboration. Remember to prioritize self-care and seek support when needed. With these strategies in place, you can navigate challenging professional relationships and break barriers to effective communication.

Mediation and Conflict Resolution Procedures

Conflict is an inevitable part of life, and it can arise in various settings, including the workplace, personal relationships, or even within communities. However, conflicts should not be feared or avoided but rather seen as opportunities for growth and improved relationships. To effectively navigate conflicts, mediation, and conflict resolution procedures play a crucial role. In this subchapter, we will explore the significance of mediation and provide practical strategies for conflict resolution.

Mediation is a voluntary and confidential process that involves a neutral third party facilitating communication between conflicting parties. It aims to foster understanding, find common ground, and reach mutually beneficial solutions. Mediation is particularly valuable because it empowers individuals to actively participate in resolving their conflicts, rather than relying on external authorities or escalating the dispute.

One of the primary benefits of mediation is its emphasis on preserving relationships. Unlike adversarial approaches that often result in winners and losers, mediation encourages collaboration and compromise. By fostering open dialogue and active listening, mediation allows parties to express their concerns, clarify misunderstandings, and work toward a resolution that addresses everyone's needs.

To engage in effective mediation, certain conflict resolution procedures can be employed. These include setting ground rules to ensure respectful communication, identifying and acknowledging each party's interests and perspectives, and reframing the conflict as a shared problem to encourage collaboration. Mediators can employ various techniques such as brainstorming, reality testing, and problem-solving to guide the parties toward mutually satisfactory solutions.

In the workplace, mediation can be particularly beneficial for improving team dynamics, increasing productivity, and reducing stress. By providing a safe space for individuals to express their grievances and concerns, mediation can help resolve conflicts before they escalate, preserving harmony and morale within the organization.

Beyond the workplace, mediation techniques can be applied in various personal and community settings. By promoting empathy, active listening, and compromise, mediation contributes to healthier relationships, stronger communities, and improved communication skills.

Whether you are a manager, employee, community leader, or simply someone interested in enhancing your conflict resolution skills, understanding mediation and conflict resolution procedures is essential. By engaging in these practices, you can break down barriers, foster understanding, and cultivate a more harmonious environment in all areas of your life.

Chapter 8: Conflict Resolution in Community and Society

Conflict Resolution in Educational Settings

In the realm of education, conflicts are bound to arise due to the diverse backgrounds, perspectives, and goals of individuals involved. Whether it be between students, teachers, administrators, or parents, these conflicts can hinder the learning process and create a negative atmosphere. Therefore, it is crucial to address and resolve conflicts effectively in educational settings to promote a harmonious learning environment and foster positive relationships.

This subchapter aims to provide strategies for conflict resolution specifically tailored to educational settings. It is an essential resource for everyone involved in the education system, including students, teachers, administrators, and parents. By mastering the art of conflict resolution, individuals can enhance communication skills, build empathy, and create a more inclusive and supportive learning community.

The chapter begins by highlighting the importance of conflict resolution in educational settings. It emphasizes the negative impact of unresolved conflicts on academic performance, social relationships, and emotional well-being. By understanding the significance of conflict resolution, individuals are motivated to actively engage in the process and seek mutually beneficial solutions.

Next, the subchapter explores various conflict resolution strategies applicable to educational settings. These strategies include active listening, effective communication, brainstorming, negotiation, and mediation. Each strategy is explained in detail, accompanied by real-life examples and practical tips. The content also highlights the importance of empathy, respect, and open-mindedness in conflict resolution.

Moreover, the subchapter addresses the different types of conflicts prevalent in educational settings, such as student-student conflicts, student-teacher conflicts, and parent-teacher conflicts. It provides specific guidance on how to approach and resolve each type of conflict effectively, taking into account the unique dynamics and power imbalances involved.

Lastly, the subchapter emphasizes the role of preventive measures in conflict resolution. It discusses the importance of fostering a positive school culture, promoting inclusivity, and teaching conflict resolution skills from an early age. By creating a proactive environment that values open communication and respect, conflicts can be minimized, and a sense of community can be fostered.

In conclusion, conflict resolution is vital in educational settings to ensure a positive and conducive learning environment. By implementing the strategies and techniques mentioned in this subchapter, individuals can effectively resolve conflicts, improve communication skills, and cultivate harmonious relationships. Ultimately, this subchapter serves as a comprehensive guide for everyone involved in education, providing valuable insights and tools for successful conflict resolution.

Conflict Resolution in Neighborhoods and Communities

Introduction

In today's fast-paced world, conflicts are bound to arise in neighborhoods and communities. Whether it's a disagreement between neighbors, a clash of interests in a community project, or a misunderstanding among community members, conflicts can disrupt the harmony and hinder progress. However, with effective conflict resolution strategies, these conflicts can be resolved peacefully, fostering stronger relationships and a sense of unity within the neighborhood or community.

Understanding Conflict

Before delving into conflict resolution strategies, it is important to understand what conflict is. Conflict arises when there is a clash of interests, values, or needs between individuals or groups. It can be caused by a lack of communication, differing perspectives, or even external factors that impact the community as a whole. Recognizing the signs of conflict and understanding its root causes are crucial steps towards finding a resolution.

Effective Communication as a Key

One of the fundamental pillars of conflict resolution is effective communication. By promoting open and honest dialogue, individuals can express their concerns, listen to others, and seek common ground. Active listening and empathy play vital roles in this process, as they enable individuals to understand each other's perspectives and find mutually beneficial solutions. Additionally, clear and respectful communication helps prevent misunderstandings and allows for the smooth resolution of conflicts.

Mediation and Collaboration

In some cases, conflicts may escalate to a point where mediation is necessary. Mediation involves a neutral third party, such as a trained mediator or community leader, who facilitates communication between conflicting parties. Mediators help identify common interests and guide the parties towards finding a resolution that satisfies everyone involved. Collaboration is another powerful tool in conflict resolution, as it encourages individuals to work together towards a shared goal, pooling their ideas and resources.

Building a Supportive Community

Creating a supportive community is essential for effective conflict resolution. By fostering a sense of belonging and inclusivity, community members are more likely to approach conflicts with a cooperative mindset. Encouraging community engagement, organizing social events, and establishing platforms for dialogue can all contribute to building a stronger and more united neighborhood or community.

Conclusion

Conflict resolution in neighborhoods and communities is a necessary skill that everyone can benefit from. By prioritizing effective communication, promoting mediation and collaboration, and building a supportive community, conflicts can be resolved peacefully, leading to a harmonious and thriving environment. Breaking barriers and finding common ground are essential strategies for conflict resolution, enabling individuals to communicate better not only in their neighborhoods and communities but also in their workplaces and beyond.

Conflict Resolution in Social Movements and Activism

In the realm of social movements and activism, conflicts are not uncommon. When individuals with diverse perspectives come together to work towards a common goal, disagreements and clashes are bound to arise. However, effective conflict resolution is crucial for the success and sustainability of any movement. This subchapter explores various strategies for navigating conflicts within social movements and activism, providing valuable insights for anyone involved in these areas.

One of the key aspects of conflict resolution in social movements is fostering open and respectful communication. As activists, it is essential to create an environment where all voices are heard and valued. This involves active listening, empathy, and the willingness to understand different viewpoints. By acknowledging diverse perspectives, conflicts can be transformed into opportunities for growth and learning, rather than sources of division.

Another crucial strategy for conflict resolution is the establishment of effective decision-making processes. Social movements often consist of diverse groups with differing priorities and agendas. By implementing democratic decision-making mechanisms, such as consensus-building or voting, conflicts can be resolved through collective decision-making. This ensures that everyone has a stake in the movement's direction, reducing the chances of internal disputes.

Moreover, it is vital to recognize and address power imbalances within social movements. Hierarchies and power dynamics can lead to conflicts and marginalization of certain voices. By actively working towards inclusivity and empowering marginalized groups, conflicts arising from power imbalances can be mitigated. This requires creating safe spaces for open dialogue, promoting diversity in leadership roles, and actively seeking out and addressing issues of privilege and oppression.

Additionally, conflict resolution in social movements often involves strategic negotiation and compromise. While it is important to stay steadfast in the pursuit of justice, compromise can be a valuable tool for resolving conflicts and building alliances. Finding common ground and seeking win-win solutions can help maintain unity and effectiveness within social movements.

Lastly, conflict resolution in social movements requires ongoing reflection and learning. It is essential to continuously evaluate the effectiveness of strategies and approaches, and adapt accordingly. By fostering a culture of learning and self-reflection, social movements can constantly improve their conflict resolution practices and create lasting change.

In conclusion, conflict resolution is an integral part of social movements and activism. By prioritizing open communication, effective decision-making, addressing power imbalances, strategic negotiation, and continued learning, conflicts within social movements can be transformed into opportunities for growth and unity. The strategies discussed in this subchapter provide valuable insights for individuals involved in social movements and activism, helping them navigate conflicts and build stronger, more inclusive movements.

Conflict Resolution in International Relations

In today's interconnected world, conflicts between nations have become increasingly complex and challenging to resolve. The subchapter on "Conflict Resolution in International Relations" from the book "Breaking Barriers: Strategies for Conflict Resolution and Effective Communication" aims to provide valuable insights and practical strategies for everyone interested in understanding and addressing these global disputes.

International relations encompass diplomatic negotiations, economic agreements, and political interactions between nations. Conflicts in this realm can arise due to various reasons such as territorial disputes, ideological differences, or competition for resources. Resolving these conflicts requires a deep understanding of the underlying issues and a willingness to engage in open dialogue.

The subchapter begins by emphasizing the importance of effective communication in conflict resolution. It explores how miscommunication and misunderstandings often escalate tensions and hinder progress. By enhancing our communication skills, we can bridge the gap between conflicting parties and foster understanding and compromise.

The subchapter then delves into various strategies for conflict resolution in the international arena. It highlights the significance of diplomacy and negotiation as essential tools for resolving disputes peacefully. Through diplomatic channels, nations can engage in dialogue, present their perspectives, and work towards finding mutually beneficial solutions.

Additionally, the subchapter emphasizes the importance of involving neutral third parties, such as mediators or international organizations, in conflict resolution processes. These impartial actors can facilitate negotiations, mediate between conflicting parties, and provide valuable insights to reach a fair and sustainable resolution.

Furthermore, the subchapter explores the role of international law and institutions in conflict resolution. It highlights the significance of adhering to international norms and agreements to prevent and resolve conflicts. By upholding the rule of law and engaging in multilateral cooperation, nations can navigate complex disputes with a framework that promotes stability and justice.

Lastly, the subchapter acknowledges that conflict resolution in international relations is a complex and ongoing process. It encourages readers to stay informed about global affairs, foster intercultural understanding, and actively engage in promoting peace and cooperation on both individual and collective levels.

"Conflict Resolution in International Relations" is an essential subchapter in the book "Breaking Barriers: Strategies for Conflict Resolution and Effective Communication." It provides valuable insights and practical strategies for everyone interested in understanding and addressing global conflicts. By fostering effective communication, engaging in diplomacy, involving neutral third parties, upholding international law, and promoting peace, individuals can contribute to a more harmonious and interconnected world.

Chapter 9: Strategies for Self-Reflection and Personal Growth

Identifying Personal Communication Patterns

In the quest for effective communication, it is essential to recognize that each individual has their unique communication style and patterns. Understanding these patterns not only allows us to enhance our own communication skills but also enables us to build stronger relationships with others. By identifying personal communication patterns, we can bridge the gap between misunderstandings and conflicts, leading to more harmonious interactions in all areas of life.

One key aspect of recognizing personal communication patterns is self-awareness. Taking the time to reflect on how we communicate can provide valuable insights into our strengths and weaknesses. Are we assertive or passive in our communication? Do we tend to avoid conflict or address it head-on? Are we good listeners or do we dominate conversations? Identifying such patterns helps us understand our default communication style and allows us to make conscious efforts to improve our communication skills.

Another vital aspect is understanding the impact of non-verbal communication. Our body language, facial expressions, and tone of voice often convey more than our words. By observing these non-verbal cues in ourselves and others, we can gain deeper insights into our communication patterns. Are we aware of the message our body language sends? Do we pay attention to the non-verbal cues of others? Recognizing and interpreting these non-verbal signals enhances our ability to communicate effectively and empathetically.

Furthermore, identifying personal communication patterns involves recognizing the role of cultural and social influences. Different cultures and social contexts have unique communication norms and expectations. Being aware of these differences helps us adapt our communication style to suit diverse audiences. It also enables us to avoid misunderstandings and potential conflicts arising from misinterpretations.

To identify personal communication patterns, it is beneficial to seek feedback from others. Asking trusted friends, colleagues, or family members for their observations provides valuable perspectives on our communication style. Others may notice patterns that we are unaware of, such as repetitive phrases, interruptions, or a tendency to avoid certain topics. By incorporating this feedback into our self-reflection, we can refine our communication patterns and become more effective communicators.

In conclusion, identifying personal communication patterns is a crucial step towards improving our communication skills and fostering better relationships. Through self-awareness, understanding non-verbal communication, considering cultural influences, and seeking feedback, we can gain valuable insights into our communication style. By recognizing and addressing our communication patterns, we can break down barriers, resolve conflicts, and communicate better at work and beyond. Remember, effective communication is a lifelong journey, and by continuously refining our skills, we can achieve greater success and fulfillment in all aspects of our lives.

Developing Emotional Resilience

In today's fast-paced and ever-changing world, it is crucial for everyone to develop emotional resilience. Life is full of challenges, setbacks, and conflicts that can easily leave us feeling overwhelmed and drained. However, by cultivating emotional resilience, we can navigate these hurdles with grace, bounce back from adversity, and maintain a positive outlook.

Emotional resilience is the ability to adapt and cope with stress, adversity, and emotional challenges. It is not about suppressing emotions or pretending that everything is fine. Instead, it is about developing the skills and mindset to effectively manage our emotions and bounce back from difficult situations.

One of the key aspects of developing emotional resilience is self-awareness. By understanding our own emotions, triggers, and coping mechanisms, we can better navigate challenging situations. This self-awareness allows us to recognize when we are experiencing stress or negative emotions and take proactive steps to address them. Whether it is through relaxation techniques, seeking support from others, or engaging in activities that bring us joy, self-awareness empowers us to take control of our emotional well-being.

Another important skill in developing emotional resilience is effective communication. Conflict resolution and effective communication go hand in hand, as they both require being able to express ourselves assertively while also being receptive to the perspectives of others. By developing good communication skills, we can navigate conflicts more effectively, maintain healthy relationships, and reduce stress.

Furthermore, building a strong support network is vital for developing emotional resilience. Surrounding ourselves with people who uplift and support us can greatly enhance our ability to bounce back from challenges. Whether it is seeking advice or simply having someone to listen, a support network provides us with the emotional support we need during difficult times.

Lastly, developing emotional resilience requires practicing self-care. Taking care of our physical, mental, and emotional well-being is essential for building resilience. Engaging in activities that promote relaxation, such as exercise, meditation, or hobbies, can help us recharge and reduce stress levels.

In conclusion, developing emotional resilience is a crucial skill for everyone, regardless of their niche or role in life. By cultivating self-awareness, effective communication, building a support network, and practicing self-care, we can develop the resilience needed to navigate the challenges of life with ease. Remember, it is not about avoiding difficult situations, but rather about building the skills and mindset to bounce back stronger and more resilient than ever before.

Self-Care and Stress Management

In our fast-paced and demanding world, taking care of ourselves should be a top priority. The subchapter on "Self-Care and Stress Management" in the book "Breaking Barriers: Strategies for Conflict Resolution and Effective Communication" aims to provide practical and effective tips for everyone to navigate the challenges of daily life with ease and resilience.

In the hustle and bustle of our busy lives, it's easy to get overwhelmed and neglect our own well-being. However, self-care is not a luxury; it is a necessity. When we take care of ourselves, we become better equipped to handle stress, communicate effectively, and resolve conflicts in a productive manner.

This subchapter explores various aspects of self-care, starting with the importance of establishing healthy boundaries. By setting clear boundaries in our personal and professional lives, we can protect our time, energy, and emotional well-being. It also delves into the significance of self-reflection and self-awareness, highlighting the benefits of taking time to understand our own needs, triggers, and limitations.

Additionally, the subchapter provides practical strategies for managing stress. It emphasizes the value of finding healthy coping mechanisms such as exercise, meditation, and hobbies. It also encourages readers to prioritize self-care activities and create a balanced routine that includes relaxation and rejuvenation.

Furthermore, "Self-Care and Stress Management" explores the connection between self-care and effective communication. It emphasizes the importance of self-compassion and self-acceptance in building healthy relationships and resolving conflicts. By taking the time to care for ourselves, we cultivate the inner peace and resilience necessary to communicate better at work and beyond.

This subchapter is a valuable resource for everyone, from busy professionals striving to excel in their careers to individuals seeking to improve their personal relationships. It provides practical guidance and actionable tips that can be implemented in daily life, promoting a healthier, happier, and more harmonious existence.

In conclusion, "Self-Care and Stress Management" is an essential subchapter in the book "Breaking Barriers: Strategies for Conflict Resolution and Effective Communication." It serves as a comprehensive guide for everyone, offering insights into the importance of self-care, stress management, and their impact on effective communication. By prioritizing self-care, we can not only enhance our own well-being but also foster better relationships and navigate conflicts with ease.

Continuous Improvement and Lifelong Learning

In today's rapidly changing world, the need for continuous improvement and lifelong learning cannot be overstated. Regardless of your age, profession, or personal circumstances, embracing a mindset of growth and development is crucial for success and fulfillment. This subchapter explores the importance of continuous improvement and lifelong learning, providing practical strategies for achieving personal and professional growth.

The journey of continuous improvement begins with the recognition that there is always room for growth. No matter how experienced or knowledgeable you are, there are always new skills to acquire, fresh perspectives to gain, and innovative ideas to explore. By committing to lifelong learning, you open yourself up to endless possibilities and opportunities for personal and professional advancement.

One of the key benefits of continuous improvement is the ability to adapt to a rapidly changing world. Technology, industry trends, and societal norms are constantly evolving, and those who resist change may find themselves left behind. Lifelong learning allows you to stay ahead of the curve, ensuring that you can navigate challenges with confidence and embrace new opportunities with ease.

Moreover, continuous improvement fosters personal growth and fulfillment. Learning new skills and acquiring knowledge not only enhances your professional capabilities but also broadens your horizons and enriches your personal life. Whether you choose to explore a new hobby, develop a new talent, or dive into a subject you've always been curious about, the process of continuous learning brings joy and a sense of accomplishment.

To embark on a journey of continuous improvement and lifelong learning, it is essential to cultivate a growth mindset. Embrace challenges as opportunities for growth, seek feedback from others, and view setbacks as learning experiences rather than failures. Set clear goals for yourself, both short-term and long-term, and create a plan to achieve them. Explore different learning methods and resources, such as books, online courses, workshops, and mentorship programs, to find what works best for you.

Remember, continuous improvement and lifelong learning are not just reserved for the young or those pursuing specific careers. They are essential for everyone, regardless of age or occupation, who seeks personal growth, professional success, and a fulfilling life. By adopting a mindset of growth and committing to lifelong learning, you can break barriers, improve your communication skills, and achieve your fullest potential in all areas of life.

Chapter 10: Applying Conflict Resolution and Effective Communication Skills

Conflict Prevention and Early Intervention

In today's fast-paced and interconnected world, conflicts are inevitable. Whether it is at work, in our personal relationships, or within communities, conflicts can arise from differing perspectives, misunderstandings, or simply clashing personalities. However, conflicts don't have to escalate into full-blown disputes. By focusing on conflict prevention and early intervention, we can effectively address conflicts before they spiral out of control, leading to more harmonious and productive relationships.

Conflict prevention starts with open and honest communication. By encouraging dialogue and active listening, we can foster an environment where issues can be openly discussed and resolved before they escalate. It is crucial to create a safe space where individuals feel comfortable expressing their concerns and opinions without fear of judgment or retaliation. By promoting a culture of respect and understanding, conflicts can be nipped in the bud, preventing them from festering and causing further damage.

Early intervention is equally important in conflict resolution. Recognizing the signs of brewing conflicts and addressing them promptly can significantly minimize the negative impact. This requires keen observation and empathy. By understanding the underlying causes of conflicts, we can identify potential solutions or mediate discussions to prevent further escalation. It is vital to act swiftly and decisively to resolve conflicts before they become deeply entrenched, leading to lasting damage to relationships and productivity.

Conflict prevention and early intervention strategies are not limited to specific niches but are applicable to everyone, both in professional and personal contexts. By practicing effective communication techniques such as active listening, assertiveness, and empathy, individuals can proactively address conflicts and prevent them from becoming major disruptions in their lives. These strategies are particularly relevant in the workplace, where conflicts can hinder productivity, erode morale, and damage teamwork.

In conclusion, conflict prevention and early intervention are essential tools for maintaining healthy relationships and fostering a positive environment. By prioritizing open and honest communication, recognizing the signs of conflicts, and taking prompt action, we can minimize the negative impact of conflicts and promote better understanding and cooperation. Whether at work or in our personal lives, these strategies are invaluable in breaking barriers and achieving effective communication that leads to conflict resolution and harmonious relationships.

Resolving Conflicts in Real-Life Scenarios

Conflicts are an inevitable part of life, occurring in various settings such as the workplace, relationships, and even within ourselves. However, the way we handle conflicts can make a significant difference in the outcomes we achieve. In this subchapter, we will explore strategies for resolving conflicts in real-life scenarios, equipping you with the skills to break barriers and foster effective communication.

When faced with a conflict, the first step is to approach it with an open mind and a willingness to understand the perspectives of all parties involved. This empathetic mindset allows us to acknowledge the emotions and concerns of others, creating a foundation for constructive dialogue. Active listening plays a crucial role in this process, as it demonstrates respect and validates the feelings of those involved.

One effective strategy for conflict resolution is the use of "I" statements. By expressing our own emotions and needs using statements such as "I feel" or "I need," we avoid blaming or accusing the other person. This approach encourages open and honest communication, fostering a sense of mutual understanding and collaboration.

Another valuable technique is finding common ground. Identifying shared goals or interests can help shift the focus from conflict to cooperation. By emphasizing the importance of the relationship or the desired outcome, we can create a sense of unity and work together towards a resolution.

In some cases, conflicts may escalate and require mediation. In such situations, a neutral third party can assist in facilitating communication and finding a middle ground. This mediator should be skilled in active listening, problem-solving, and maintaining a neutral stance. Their purpose is to guide the conversation and ensure that all parties have an opportunity to be heard.

It is essential to remember that conflicts are not always resolved immediately. Patience and perseverance are key qualities to cultivate during the resolution process. By remaining calm and composed, we can prevent conflicts from escalating further and create an atmosphere of trust and respect.

In conclusion, conflicts are an inevitable part of life, but by adopting effective strategies for conflict resolution, we can break barriers and foster better communication. Approaching conflicts with an open mind, using "I" statements, finding common ground, and seeking mediation when necessary are all tools that can lead to successful resolutions. Ultimately, by resolving conflicts in real-life scenarios, we can enhance our relationships, improve our work environments, and create a more harmonious society.

Effective Communication in Challenging Situations

In today's fast-paced and interconnected world, effective communication has become an indispensable skill for success in both personal and professional realms. However, it is in challenging situations that the true power of effective communication is put to the test. Whether it is a conflict at work, a disagreement with a loved one, or a difficult conversation with a client, being able to communicate effectively in challenging situations can make all the difference in resolving conflicts, building stronger relationships, and achieving desired outcomes.

In this subchapter, we will delve into the strategies and techniques that can help everyone navigate challenging situations and communicate better, both at work and beyond. These strategies are derived from the principles outlined in the book "Breaking Barriers: Strategies for Conflict Resolution and Effective Communication," which aims to equip individuals with the tools they need to overcome communication barriers and achieve positive outcomes in all areas of life.

One of the key principles we will explore is the art of active listening. In challenging situations, it is crucial to truly understand the perspective of the other person involved. Active listening involves not only hearing their words but also empathizing with their emotions and underlying concerns. By actively listening, we can foster a sense of understanding and create an environment where both parties feel heard and acknowledged.

Another essential strategy is the use of assertive communication. Assertiveness allows individuals to express their thoughts, feelings, and needs in a clear and respectful manner. It helps to avoid misunderstandings, build trust, and find mutually beneficial solutions. We will explore techniques for practicing assertive communication, such as using "I" statements, maintaining a calm demeanor, and focusing on the issue at hand rather than personal attacks.

Furthermore, we will delve into the importance of non-verbal communication in challenging situations. Non-verbal cues, such as body language and facial expressions, can convey powerful messages and influence the outcome of a conversation. Understanding and effectively utilizing non-verbal communication can help individuals project confidence, establish rapport, and defuse tense situations.

Lastly, we will discuss the significance of emotional intelligence in challenging situations. Emotional intelligence involves recognizing and managing our own emotions, as well as understanding and empathizing with the emotions of others. By developing emotional intelligence, individuals can navigate challenging conversations with sensitivity, empathy, and a focus on finding common ground.

In conclusion, effective communication in challenging situations is a vital skill that everyone should strive to develop. By employing strategies such as active listening, assertive communication, non-verbal cues, and emotional intelligence, individuals can improve their ability to communicate effectively in all areas of life. "Breaking Barriers: Strategies for Conflict Resolution and Effective Communication" provides a comprehensive guide for individuals seeking to enhance their communication skills and overcome barriers to success. Whether in the workplace or in personal relationships, the principles outlined in this book offer valuable insights and practical tools for communicating better at work and beyond.

Conflict Resolution and Effective Communication in the Digital Age

In today's digital age, where communication is more instantaneous and widespread than ever before, conflict resolution and effective communication have become essential skills for everyone. Whether you are navigating workplace dynamics, maintaining personal relationships, or engaging with others online, the ability to resolve conflicts and communicate effectively is crucial for success and fulfillment.

The digital age has both facilitated and complicated our communication processes. While it has opened up new avenues for connecting with others, it has also presented unique challenges. Misunderstandings can easily arise due to the absence of non-verbal cues, tone, and facial expressions that are typically present in face-to-face interactions. Therefore, learning how to effectively communicate and resolve conflicts in this digital landscape is paramount.

The subchapter "Conflict Resolution and Effective Communication in the Digital Age" explores the strategies and techniques that can help individuals navigate these challenges and achieve positive outcomes in their interactions. It offers practical advice and actionable tips to enhance communication skills in various contexts, including the workplace and personal relationships.

One of the key aspects addressed in this subchapter is the importance of active listening. In the digital age, it is easy to get distracted or misinterpret messages, leading to conflict. By actively listening and seeking clarification when needed, individuals can avoid misunderstandings and build stronger relationships.

Additionally, this subchapter delves into the significance of empathy and understanding in conflict resolution. It highlights the value of taking the time to understand others' perspectives and emotions, even in digital interactions. By fostering empathy, individuals can bridge gaps, find common ground, and resolve conflicts more effectively.

Furthermore, the subchapter explores the role of technology in conflict resolution and communication. It discusses the potential pitfalls of relying solely on digital platforms and emphasizes the importance of face-to-face or video communication whenever possible. It also provides guidance on leveraging technology to enhance communication, such as using collaborative tools and virtual platforms for effective teamwork.

"Conflict Resolution and Effective Communication in the Digital Age" is a valuable resource for everyone seeking to improve their communication skills and navigate conflicts in the ever-evolving digital landscape. By implementing the strategies and techniques outlined in this subchapter, readers can break barriers, foster understanding, and build stronger connections in both personal and professional spheres.

Chapter 11: Conclusion

Recap of Key Strategies for Conflict Resolution and Effective Communication

In this subchapter, we will recap some of the key strategies for conflict resolution and effective communication that have been discussed in the book "Breaking Barriers: Strategies for Conflict Resolution and Effective Communication." These strategies are applicable to everyone, regardless of their professional or personal backgrounds. Whether you are looking to improve your communication skills at work or in your personal relationships, these strategies will help you navigate conflicts and communicate more effectively.

1. Active Listening: One of the most important skills in effective communication is active listening. This involves paying full attention to the speaker, maintaining eye contact, and providing verbal and non-verbal cues to show that you are engaged in the conversation. Active listening helps to build trust and understanding, and it allows you to respond more effectively to the speaker's needs.

2. Empathy and Understanding: To resolve conflicts, it is crucial to put yourself in the other person's shoes. Show empathy and understanding towards their perspective, even if you disagree with them. This will help create a safe space for open and honest communication, fostering a more productive resolution.

3. Effective Verbal and Non-Verbal Communication: Communication is not just about the words we use; it also involves our tone, body language, and facial expressions. Pay attention to your own non-verbal cues and be mindful of how they may be perceived by others. Use clear and concise language to express your thoughts and feelings, avoiding aggressive or defensive tones.

4. Conflict Resolution Strategies: When conflicts arise, it is essential to approach them with a problem-solving mindset. Identify the root cause of the conflict, and focus on finding a mutually beneficial solution. Use techniques such as active listening, compromise, and negotiation to reach a resolution that satisfies all parties involved.

5. Emotional Intelligence: Developing emotional intelligence is crucial for effective communication and conflict resolution. This involves

recognizing and managing your own emotions, as well as understanding and empathizing with the emotions of others. By being aware of your emotions and their impact on your communication, you can respond more effectively to conflicts.

By applying these key strategies for conflict resolution and effective communication, you can improve your relationships, both personally and professionally. Remember that effective communication is a continuous process that requires practice and self-reflection. With dedication and effort, you can break barriers and build stronger connections with others.

Encouragement for Continued Practice and Growth

In the journey towards effective communication and conflict resolution, it is crucial to understand that true mastery is not achieved overnight. It requires continuous practice, dedication, and a willingness to embrace growth. This subchapter aims to provide encouragement to everyone, regardless of their background or profession, on their path to becoming better communicators and conflict resolvers.

Simply said, communicating better at work and beyond is a skill that can be honed and improved upon with time. Just like any other skill, it requires patience and persistence. Remember that even the most skilled communicators started from scratch and faced their fair share of challenges along the way. So, don't be discouraged if you stumble or make mistakes. Each setback is an opportunity for growth and learning.

One of the key aspects of continued practice and growth is self-awareness. Take the time to reflect on your communication style and patterns. Identify areas where you excel and areas where you can improve. By understanding your strengths and weaknesses, you can tailor your practice sessions to address specific areas of improvement.

Another essential element is seeking feedback from others. Don't be afraid to ask for constructive criticism from colleagues, mentors, or friends. Their insights can be invaluable in helping you identify blind spots and provide guidance for improvement. Embrace feedback as a gift, as it brings you closer to becoming a more effective communicator.

It is also important to remember that growth is not a linear process. There will be ups and downs, moments of frustration, and times when you may feel like giving up. During these challenging times, it is crucial to stay motivated and remind yourself of the reasons why you embarked on this journey. Surround yourself with supportive individuals who will cheer you on and provide encouragement when you need it most.

Lastly, celebrate your progress along the way. Recognize and acknowledge the milestones you achieve, no matter how small they may seem. This will boost your confidence and reinforce your commitment to continued practice and growth.

In conclusion, regardless of your background or profession, becoming a better communicator and conflict resolver is within your grasp. Embrace the journey, practice consistently, seek feedback, stay motivated, and celebrate your progress. Remember, every step forward is a step towards breaking barriers and achieving effective communication in all areas of life.

Recommended Resources for Conflict Resolution and Effective Communication

In today's fast-paced world, effective communication and conflict resolution skills are more important than ever. Whether you are navigating workplace dynamics, managing personal relationships, or simply seeking to improve your overall communication abilities, having the right resources at your disposal can make a significant difference. This subchapter aims to provide a curated list of recommended resources that can help you break barriers and master the art of conflict resolution and effective communication.

1. "Crucial Conversations: Tools for Talking When Stakes Are High" by Kerry Patterson, Joseph Grenny, Ron McMillan, and Al Switzler. This book is a must-read for anyone looking to enhance their communication skills. It offers practical techniques and strategies to navigate difficult conversations, manage emotions, and achieve positive outcomes.

2. "Difficult Conversations: How to Discuss What Matters Most" by Douglas Stone, Bruce Patton, and Sheila Heen. This resource provides a step-by-step approach to handling tough conversations with confidence and empathy. It offers invaluable insights into understanding different perspectives and finding common ground.

3. "Nonviolent Communication: A Language of Life" by Marshall B. Rosenberg. This classic book introduces the concept of nonviolent communication, which focuses on expressing needs and resolving conflicts peacefully. It provides practical tools to foster understanding and empathy in any situation.

4. "Getting to Yes: Negotiating Agreement Without Giving In" by Roger Fisher and William Ury. This resource is an essential guide for mastering the art of negotiation. It offers a principled approach to reaching mutually beneficial agreements, emphasizing the importance of separating people from the problem.

5. "Emotional Intelligence 2.0" by Travis Bradberry and Jean Greaves. This book explores the crucial role of emotional intelligence in effective communication. It provides strategies to enhance self-awareness, manage emotions, and foster better relationships.

6. Websites and Online Courses: Explore platforms like Coursera, Udemy, and LinkedIn Learning for a wide range of online courses on conflict resolution and effective communication. These platforms offer flexibility and convenience, allowing you to learn at your own pace and explore specific topics of interest.

Remember, effective communication and conflict resolution are skills that can be learned and improved upon with practice and the right resources. By investing in your personal growth and development in these areas, you can break barriers, strengthen relationships, and achieve success in all aspects of your life.

Worksheets and Exercises for Skill Development

In order to become effective communicators and conflict-resolution experts, it is important to practice and develop our skills. This subchapter provides a variety of worksheets and exercises that will help you enhance your communication abilities and overcome barriers to effective communication. Whether you are a professional looking to improve workplace interactions or an individual striving for better personal relationships, these exercises are designed for everyone seeking to communicate better at work and beyond.

1.   Active   Listening   Exercise: Active listening is a fundamental skill for effective communication. This exercise involves pairs of participants taking turns to speak while the other actively listens. The listener must then summarize and reflect on what the speaker has said, demonstrating their understanding and active engagement.

2.   Conflict   Resolution   Scenario   Worksheet: Conflicts are inevitable, but they can be resolved in a positive and constructive manner. This worksheet presents various conflict scenarios, where you can analyze the situation, identify the underlying issues, and devise strategies for resolution. By practicing conflict resolution techniques, you will be better equipped to handle challenging situations.

3.   Non-Verbal   Communication   Analysis: Non-verbal cues play a significant role in communication. Through this exercise, you will examine different non-verbal expressions, such as facial expressions, body language, and tone of voice. By analyzing these cues, you will gain a deeper understanding of how non-verbal communication impacts the overall message being conveyed.

4.   Empathy   Building   Activity: Empathy is crucial in conflict resolution and effective communication. This activity involves participants sharing personal experiences and feelings, allowing others to listen and respond with empathy. By practicing empathy, you will develop a greater understanding of others' perspectives and build stronger connections.

5.   Effective   Feedback   Exercise: Giving and receiving feedback is essential for personal and professional growth. This exercise focuses on providing constructive feedback in a

supportive manner. Participants will practice giving feedback using the "I" statements technique, emphasizing their own feelings and observations rather than making assumptions or judgments.

These worksheets and exercises are just a sample of the tools you will find in "Breaking Barriers: Strategies for Conflict Resolution and Effective Communication." By actively engaging in these activities, you will develop the necessary skills to communicate better at work and in all areas of your life. Remember, effective communication is a lifelong journey, and the more you practice, the more confident and successful you will become in breaking barriers and resolving conflicts.